LEVEL TWO
Reading with help

Ripley® Readers

Learning to read. Reading to learn!

LEVEL ONE Sounding It Out Preschool-Kindergarten
For kids who know their alphabet and are starting to sound out words.

learning sight words • beginning reading • sounding out words

LEVEL TWO Reading with Help Preschool-Grade 1
For kids who know sight words and are learning to sound out new words.

expanding vocabulary • building confidence • sounding out bigger words

LEVEL THREE Independent Reading Grades 1-3
For kids who are beginning to read on their own.

introducing paragraphs • challenging vocabulary • reading for comprehension

LEVEL FOUR Chapters Grades 2-4
For confident readers who enjoy a mixture of images and story.

reading for learning • more complex content • feeding curiosity

Ripley Readers Designed to help kids build their reading skills and confidence at any level, this program offers a variety of fun, entertaining, and unbelievable topics to interest even the most reluctant readers. With stories and information that will spark their curiosity, each book will motivate them to start and keep reading.

Vice President, Licensing & Publishing Amanda Joiner
Editorial Manager Carrie Bolin

Editor Jordie R. Orlando
Designer Luis Fuentes
Text Carrie Bolin
Reprographics Bob Prohaska

Chief Executive Officer Andy Edwards
Chief Commercial Officer Brett Clarke
Vice President, Global Licensing &
  Consumer Products Cassie Dombrowski
Vice President, Creative Dov Ribnick
Director, Brand & Athlete Marketing Ricky Melnik
Art Director & Graphic Designer Josh Geduld
Global Accounts & Activation Manager,
  Consumer Products Andrew Hogan

Published by Ripley Publishing 2019

10 9 8 7 6 5 4 3 2 1

Copyright © 2019 Nitro Circus

ISBN: 978-1-60991-350-2

Manufactured in China in June 2019.

First Printing

Library of Congress Control Number: 2019942255

PUBLISHER'S NOTE
While every effort has been made to verify the accuracy of the entries in this book, the Publisher cannot be held responsible for any errors contained in the work. They would be glad to receive any information from readers.

WARNING
Some of the stunts and activities are undertaken by experts and should not be attempted by anyone without adequate training and supervision.

NITRO CIRCUS
BMX!

RIPLEY
PUBLISHING
a Jim Pattison Company

Nitro Circus is a group of men and women who perform stunts.

They go all over the world.

They like to do tricks no one has ever done before.

One of the sports Nitro Circus is best at is BMX.

BMX is a bike sport.

The leader of Nitro Circus
is Travis Pastrana.

He loves BMX so much
that he made his own park.

Nitro Circus riders
use helmets to stay safe.

They also use pads.

BMX riders use different bikes to do tricks.

They have thick tires,
pegs, and small frames.

Pegs help riders do cool tricks.

Some BMX riders do tricks in parks.

Others ride on the street.

But the Nitro Circus riders bike on ramps.

The best BMX riders go to the Nitro World Games.

They all do tricks to see
who will win.

BMX riders use ramps
to help them do flips.

They can jump high!

Ripley Readers

Ready for More?

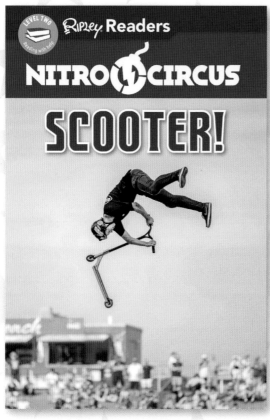

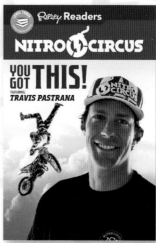

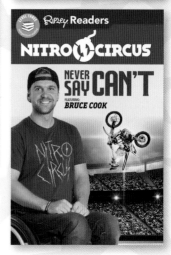

Easy to read, fun to see, and filled with amazing things, kids (even reluctant readers) will love Ripley Readers! With Nitro Circus *Scooter!*, kids aren't only learning to read, they're learning cool facts about the sport of scooter.

Learning to read. Reading to learn!

10.20